SALES

COMPENSATION

MADE

EASY

Based on decades of experience designing sales compensation plans for many companies. Includes numerous true and bizarre stories of the impact of poorly designed and well designed actual sales compensation plans

Author – Ken Pieh

Objective

To help companies develop effective sales compensation designs that are appropriate for their businesses.

Introduction

Do you have too much sales rep turnover?
Do you have lots of sales force "noise" around compensation?
Do you have some sales reps/managers making little or no money?
Do you have some sales reps/managers making huge money?
Is your sales force not performing up to expectations?
Do you have lots of sales compensation 'band-aids,' guarantees, adjustments, etc.?
Do you have difficulty calculating commissions accurately and on time?

If you are experiencing some of the above situations, your sales compensation design is probably broken and this book will help you develop an improved design.

In addition to sales compensation design recommendations; this book has references to other areas I have been deeply involved with - sales contests and quota setting.

Most chapters begin with true story(s) from personal experience. The story(s) communicate good or bad key principles in sales compensation design. I then follow the story with specific recommendations on how to avoid the problem the company experienced with their sales compensation design.

To protect the innocent (☺☺☺), I have used mountain names to represent the actual companies. I use mountain names because I enjoy mountain climbing and backpacking through them. For those of you familiar with mountain climbing nomenclature, I'll admit I'm unabashedly a "peak bagger." I enjoy summiting and descending safely, just like I enjoy a company's reaction and results when a new sales compensation design is implemented and it works. It feels great, just like summiting a mountain!

Also, never forget, there is no perfect sales compensation design. Many different designs may work for a company.

For brevity and quicker reading, going forward, I will use "sales comp" to represent "sales compensation" – fits with one of my key principles - KISS.

Quotes from Individuals I have worked with -

"Ken has done wonders for the sales comp plans at two of our companies. We would hire him to design comp plans from the outset, saving your organization the pain of trial by error. Sales people are interesting creatures and Ken knows what makes them tick!!!!!"

Tony Arnerich – CEO and CIO of Arnerich Massena Wealth Management Inc., $15B under management

"Ken helped us design our sales comp plans for three years of tremendous growth in revenues, profits and headcount and I really haven't had a serious complaint about our designs during that time. Also, sales compensation costs as a percent of revenue were reduced by over 30% during this time."

John Hironimus, Global Sales VP, Salient Surgical Technologies and, Medtronic

"Ken was a strong advocate for the field and creatively communicated compensation to the field in a simple, straight-forward way such that the field would realize total compensation was aligned to the organization's growth goals. He knew the ins and outs of sales comp design like the back of his hand. Also, he was extremely considerate and thoughtful in his approach with field personnel who often called in highly emotional states. His emotional intelligence and ability to remain calm during the onslaughts he often faced was truly an artful thing to observe."

Dan Schlewitz – National Sales VP for several companies

"Ken's redesign of what was once an awful sales compensation plan helped turn oround our company's performance and results in a dramatic way."

Joe Army – CEO - Salient Surgical Technologies and, CEO - Vapotherm

Sales Comp Made Easy (SCME) – Summary of Contents

Sales Comp Made Easy (SCME) – Table of contents - Details

Authors Background

For 25 years, I developed the sales comp designs, (including all compensation), sales contests, spiffs/bonuses, and stock award programs for a large medical device company. During this time I also designed sales comp plans for several other companies.

The sales forces ranged in size from a few reps to over 2,500 sales and service people. The company used a variety of sales channels - employees, distributors, sales agents, independent contractors, etc. Also, within each sales channel at times there were numerous variations in the sales force structures and sales comp designs.

I designed sales comp plans for start-ups, mature divisions with billions in revenue, slow and fast growing divisions. I addressed all of the issues in sales comp plans including but not limited to high and low share territories, one product sales forces, multiple product sales forces, fast and slow growing businesses, high and low margin products, large and small sales forces, multiple levels of sales management, high and low rep influence products, consumer purchased products, B 2 B products, and many other issues.

I was considered the inside expert for sales comp and sales contest related issues and consulted with OUS geographies as well.

The sales comp custom software I designed is still being used (10 years post implementation) to calculate sales comp for most of this company's U.S. sales forces.

I converted numerous sales organizations from distributors/agents/independents to direct employees with most of the "independents" becoming employees. I also built distributor organizations.

I created and led a national seminar on sales comp design for three years. Sales comp practitioners from around the country came together to discuss their issues, solutions, trends, etc. Among the participants were Coca Cola, Pfizer, Hoerscht, Abbot, 3M Medical products, Canadian and U.S. communication companies, DuPont, and many others.

After retiring early (partly to spend time in the mountains ☺☺☺), via word of mouth, (no marketing, website, etc), companies began calling me to see if I would help them with their sales comp, sales contests and other sales force related issues. Having now completed projects for several companies and reflecting on the difficulties many companies have in this area, I decided to write this book to at least offer my perspective on the how to and how not to design sales comp plans. My hope is this book will help other companies avoid the true disaster stories you will read about in this book.

Sales Comp Made Easy (SCME) is intended to help companies develop good sales comp designs, avoid "Fatal Flaws" in those designs, and offer constructive ideas on the design and communication process to have – Sales Comp Made Easy!

I own five sales comp books with a total of 1,854 pages – an average of 371 pages per book. I don't think sales comp needs to be that complex. This book may not contain everything you need, but it will certainly help with your design process and will help ensure you avoid some fatal flaws. I have used the concepts in this book many times and simply - they work.

My Commitments to my Customers

If after reading this book you consider engaging me in a sales comp design project, contest or other sales force related work, following is what I tell all my customers –

1. If you don't like what I deliver – don't pay me. Life's too short and fun to create unnecessary issues. (Thus far I have been paid for every project. This includes several I did for smaller companies on a gratis basis although at the end even those companies decided to pay me something.)
2. You will find that I take strong, and some will consider controversial positions on design approaches which are frequently used in sales comp designs. I take my positions for two reasons:
   A. I always tell my customers what I think and not what I think they want to hear. (I wrote this book the same way.)
   B. In my experience, the positions I have taken on designs have worked numerous times with many different companies and industries.
3. My experience has been that the right design ideas for most companies reside *inside* those companies, *not* in some *outside* person or entity. My entire approach is based on a premise I call **Decisions Drive Design** – *your* **decisions** in response to tons of questions will **drive *your*** design.
4. At the end of a project, I ask my customer if they were a *satisfied* or a *loyal* customer. A *Satisfied* customer would be a customer that got what they wanted or needed from me. A *loyal* customer not only got satisfaction but they also would refer me to others should the opportunity arise. Thus far, my customers have told me they were *loyal*. I assume they have been telling the truth because prior to this book, without any marketing - only word of mouth - companies continue to call me to help them with their sales comp designs. I honestly hope this book is less of a marketing tool than something that truly helps companies design effective sales comp plans.

Also, it's most likely evident to many readers that I have never written a book before. However, I don't claim my skills are in writing a book but rather this book and my skills may help companies develop improved sales comp plans. At a minimum, you'll at least get a few laughs out of what has happened at other companies.

If you would like to discuss anything about your sales comp plans, sales contests or other sales force related issues, please contact me at 612 963 3071 or kenpiehscme@gmail.com.

Again - The 5 key steps to Sales Comp Made Easy are -

1. Have achievable quotas

2. Use a simple design – *KISS*.

3. Avoid *Fatal Flaws*.

4. Don't try to do everything with sales comp.

5. Here may be a crazy new thought for you. After gathering strategic, high level input, have your first line sales managers – or a small group of them for a larger company, *along with someone* who really understands sales comp, develop the design recommendation.

There is more to sales comp design then just the above five items. However, if you will at least follow these five simple steps, it will be difficult to develop a design with fatal flaws in it and thus have the issues listed in the beginning of this book.

Chapter 1 - The Worst, Most Screwed Up, Chaos Creating, Awful, Equity Depleting Sales Comp Plan Ever

How important is a sales comp design? Read on to learn about one company that lost and then regained millions of dollars of market value by first implementing a poorly designed sales comp plan. Then, using Sales Comp Made Easy, developed a new design which dramatically helped build back the enterprise's value.

This first chapter will show you how an awful sales comp design can result in near disaster for a company. Also, a great sales comp design can have a huge positive impact on a business.

Most sales comp plans are in the middle – not awful and not great. Obviously the poorly designed plans can be improved and even average plans can be improved to either drive higher performance or reduce costs. It's up to you to decide what kind of sales comp design you have today – awful, average, or great. To some extent, your evaluation of your sales comp plan may determine how much your company will grow and or be worth. Choose wisely!

In discussing the concept of this book with the CEO of *EVEREST*, their suggestion for Chapter 1 was that I make it about "The Worst, Most Screwed Up, Chaos Creating, Awful, Sales Comp Plan Ever." I took his advice and quote and decided this first chapter would be about his company.

Amazing but true, *EVEREST* lived through an almost fatal time when the only thing wrong with the company was its sales comp design. The sales comp plan was eventually redesigned (at no incremental cost) and *EVEREST* went on to become a very successful company, purchased a few years later for one of the higher buyout values as a multiple of revenue of any company in its space after 2000.

Prior to implementation of the "The Worst, Most Screwed Up, Chaos Creating, Awful, Equity Depleting Sales Comp Plan Ever," business was great. It was one of the fastest growing companies in their state! *EVEREST* was hiring people. It was almost profitable. It had had multiple equity infusions of millions of dollars. Life was good. The sales force was happy. Reps, sales managers and sales VP's were being added to the sales force. The reps had even just had a 50% increase in their

base salary! I could go on and on and on but you get the picture.
Everything was working – products, people, pricing, etc.

Life was awesome!

Then a new "The worst sales comp design ever" was
implemented. How did I decide *EVEREST* now had the worst sales comp
design ever? Obviously I don't know if it was the worst sales comp
design ever. However, based on what *EVEREST* was valued at in the
public market place a few short years later and what it would have sold
for at that future time had the revenue growth rate remained the same
as it was during the time of the worst sales comp design ever, there
can't have been many worse sales comp plans.

(I compared the market values of *EVEREST* with similar sized
companies. Then I looked at the market values of those companies
based on revenue growth rates. The *incremental* value of *EVEREST* with
a "Sales Comp Plan Made Easy" was well over $100M and, 100% - 200%
higher value!)

As you read the rest of this chapter, remember this story is about
a real company that was exceptional prior to an awful sales comp
design, horrible when the sales comp plan had all kinds of fatal flaws in
it, and then exceptional again after the sales comp design was "Made
Easy." And some people think a sales comp design is a small,
unimportant part of a business model – nothing could be further from
the truth.

Immediately after the introduction of the worst sales comp design
ever, everything went from great to awful – not great to good but great
to *awful*. Over a five month period, the revenue growth rate slowed
from 30%+ to the high 20's, mid 20's, low 20's, high teens, and then mid
teens.

Reps and managers began leaving – Awful.
The long-term strategy became - Awful.
The CEO became - Awful.
The CFO became – Awful.
The board became – Awful.
The sales VP was no longer there – Awful.
The products became - Awful
The prices became - Awful.
Budgets were frozen – Awful.
The weather became - Awful.

One of the better descriptions I heard of what went on inside *EVEREST* when the awful sales comp plan was in place came from a senior finance individual. Their description was "One of our most important assets (the sales force) was depreciating right before my eyes. We had made major investments in growing the sales force and now it was falling apart. It seemed everything we did was like pushing a boulder uphill."

After months of deteriorating revenue growth rates, rep turnover, *NOISE* around the sales comp plan, and lots of other junk, the CEO decided the sales comp design had to be changed - at the end of the fiscal year – 7 months later. However, (using the principles and approach outlined in this book) after understanding that there were several fatal flaws in the sales comp design, hearing all the noise around sales comp from many sales force interviews, and realizing revenue growth rates would not reaccelerate until a new sales comp design was implemented, the CEO decided to implement a Sales Comp Made Easy (SCME) design within a couple months. (The tiny percentage of the sales force that was "winning" with the existing plan was allowed to be paid on the higher of the two sales comp designs – doing the right thing for the sales force when *EVEREST* had made the mistake.)

A new sales comp plan was implemented – at essentially no incremental cost to *EVEREST*! Two months later, the revenue growth rate had reaccelerated back to normal historic levels. In the second month of this reacceleration of revenues, *EVEREST* experienced the highest revenue month in the history of the company and the first month it had ever been profitable! Remember, very minimal changes in people, no change in products, prices, strategy - other than SCME. Yes, sales comp design is no small thing – it matters.

Another amazing thing was that the target payout levels and quotas were not adjusted. Part of the basis of the new sales comp plan design were the levels of numerous band-aids and quota adjustments that had been given out during the awful sales comp plan period to retain people.

One month post implementation, the national VP of sales asked his area VP's what the "noise" level was around the new sales comp plan. Their response? "There is no NOISE!!!!" Awesome. SCME had worked!

For the subsequent three years (as of this writing), the same process was used and each year the program was successful. The strategic/longer term perspective built into the design resulted in only minor changes each succeeding year.

One sign of a well-designed plan is: if the market, company, and industry don't have dramatic change, a core design should last for several years as this one did. In fact, (keeping in mind that target pay levels were not increased during this time period) the sales force almost balked at the conversations each year around – "We're going to review the sales comp plan again." Their feedback in succeeding years was "The design works, leave it alone." We made minor changes but the core remained the same.

One of the more extraordinary changes implemented in the subsequent fiscal year was that sales rep salaries were actually *reduced* by $20,000 (33%) in order to get an appropriate mix of base salary and commissions. Not one rep left due to this change. This is testimony to not only a well-designed sales comp plan, but more importantly how important culture and ethics are in an organization. The sales force trusted their sales leaders to do the right thing for the organization and throughout the troubled time. That trust was a huge factor in turning around performance.

If a sales force is always beaten down, told they can't "get it done," given unrealistic quotas, and then blamed for underperformance, its hard for that sales force to deliver. Therefore, as I will reiterate several times in this book, having achievable plans is a must for a sales comp plan to be successful.

Finally, a key goal of a growing organization is to reduce commissions as percent of revenue over time. This was accomplished at *EVEREST* by lowering this metric by over 30% during the next 3 years – while adding 100 people to the sales force!

The Five Easy Steps used to help turn around *EVEREST* –

1. Have achievable quotas. (Quotas weren't changed with the initial implementation of SCME.)
2. We used a simple design – KISS. One quote – "It was elegantly simple."
3. We avoided Fatal Flaws.
4. Didn't try to do everything with sales compensation.
5. After gathering strategic, high level input, we had a small group of first line sales managers, *along with someone* who really understood sales comp, develop the design recommendation. It worked!

There is more to sales comp design then the above but if you at least follow these five simple steps, it will be difficult to develop a design with fatal flaws in it and have the issues listed on the first page of this book.

The next five chapters cover the five key principles in developing a Sales Comp Made Easy design.

The Five Simple, Key Steps to a Successful Sales Compensation Plan

Chapter 2 - Step 1 - Have Achievable Quotas

More important than sales comp design is to have achievable quotas.

A CFO developed *MT. RAINIER'S* sales comp plan that not only had unrealistic quotas but they also built in the concept that before any commissions were paid, a rep had to achieve 90% of quota in each of 5 different commission categories! This would be called perfection! Crazy!

The design lasted for two quarters of terrible performance. It was surprising it lasted that long. Reps left, sales managers were up in arms, the entire sales force was de-motivated, etc. In the sales force and even inside *Mt. Rainier,* people had a hard time coming up with anything good to say about anything to do with the company.

Effective with the third quarter, the CFO of *MT. RAINIER* relented and implemented a design that only required 3 of 5 elements to be at a minimum threshold (75%) for any commissions to be paid. Quotas were not reduced.

Performance improved slightly in the back half of the year and then the entire plan was redesigned the following year.

Post Mortem – The commission cost savings goal of the CFO was more than entirely wiped out by the lost revenue due to a demoralized sales force. The sad thing is this all could have been avoided with a sales comp plan that had been "MADE EASY" with achievable quotas.

Another true story – *MATTERHORN* used quotas that far exceeded the potential of their sales force to achieve. What happened? They implemented an average of three spiffs per year (3 out of 4 quarters/year) that cost the company extra commission dollars. Also, tons of loading was required at the end of each quarter, reps and managers continually whined, rep turnover increased, and the sales force became demoralized.

At the same time, another company in the same industry implemented quotas that were more reflective of the industry's growth rate and stole share from the company that was unwilling to use appropriate quotas.

It took several years before the company with quotas that were too high to start regaining share and this only happened after their quotas were set at more realistic levels.

For Sales Comp Made Easy, you need achievable quotas!

You want your sales force waking up as often as possible (everyday!) thinking, "I can get to or above quota." Many companies set unrealistic quotas because the thought process is that sales people will achieve any quota they are given.   This is simply not true. If quotas are unrealistic, noise, turnover, whining, band-aids, all sorts of non-productive things go on, including comments that the sales comp design is the problem.

Another reason unrealistic goals are set is to protect the company from spending too much money on sales comp. A well-designed sales comp plan doesn't need protection from the unit/revenue quota setting process. Also, throw out the concept that you are spending money on sales comp. When you think about your sales comp expense line, think of it as one of the most important investments you will ever make in your company – not just another cost.

Consider pole vaulters. When they are going for a personal best, they don't raise the bar 5 – 10 feet higher than they have ever leapt before. They raise the bar an amount they think they can achieve. Companies should do the same – have plans the sales force thinks they can beat and they just might do that!

Bottom line, you can pay 100% of revenue to reps and it won't be motivational if the quotas are too high.

For a sales comp plan made easy, you need achievable quotas.

The Five Simple, Key Steps to a Successful Sales Compensation Plan

Chapter 3 – Step 2 – KISS – Keep it Simple Stupid

Without simplicity, you can never have Sales Comp Made Easy. "K2" had two major products to sell to two different call points in hospitals. In trying to be simple, HR designed a sales comp plan that was based on what I call a "grid" concept. The idea was that as performance vs. quota in the two product lines improved, more commissions would be earned. The problem was that if a rep performed very well in only one product line, the grid design prevented that rep from earning very much in total commissions.

The results were that no one understood the design, the sales managers didn't like communicating the design (which showed as they rolled out the design to their reps), performance was less than expected for both product lines, and there was tons of grumbling.

Post mortem – The design lasted for one year of terrible performance. In the subsequent year, a collaborative effort between sales, HR and a knowledgeable sales comp plan designer developed a design that separated the performance of the two product lines. Commissions were earned on each products performance – individually. Performance in both product lines improved.

Think about the competing objectives that come to bear on sales comp designs.

Finance wants profit, the highest margin products sold at the highest price, no obsolescence in the launch of a new product, increased leverage in compensation over-time, etc.

Sales wants faster revenue growth, plan achievement every month, quarter and year, by everybody in the sales force, no sandbagging nor stuffing.

Marketing wants the right product mix and plan performance for all products.

HR/Legal wants a "fair" program, no incentives to do the "wrong" things with customers.

Sales reps and sales managers want to maximize their income and cash flow, know what they make on every sale, have huge bonuses over plan, and have no risk.

Thinking of all the different opinions/wants above, how can a sales comp plan do all the above? It can't. *Many* things have to be compromised. Bottom line, if the sales force is achieving its main goals, other objectives have to be accomplished by sales management direction.

KISS – It simply - WORKS!

The Five Simple, Key Steps to a Successful Sales Compensation Plan

Chapter 4 - Step 3 - Avoid Fatal Flaws

How does this actual sales comp design plan sound? 50% of revenue paid to reps! *MT. Hood* had a sales comp design that required exceptional growth but commensurately had extraordinary above-quota payout rates – 50% of revenue! Reps thought this was exciting - 50% of everything they sold would be paid to them in commissions. The problem was that only a few reps could achieve the threshold that was required to get into the extraordinary payout rates. Most of the reps weren't earning any commissions at all and became demoralized, the noise level became excessive around compensation, reps and managers began leaving *MT HOOD,* and many others mentally shut down. One quote directly from a rep – "The most destructive compensation plan ever – there was no middle class." Actually there was no lower class either.

For *MT. ADAMs*, the revenue quota was $250,000. At 99% of quota, a rep would have $247,500 in revenue and earn $20,000 in commissions. However, if they sold just $2,500 more for a total of $250,000 in revenue, the rep would increase their commissions by $5,000 to $25,000. $5,000 in commissions for $2,500 in revenue – a 200% commission rate! – not a great deal for *Mt. ADAMS*! Commissions of twice the revenue generated. Crazy! Not only was this design crazy, the real issue for *MT. ADAMS* was that if a rep could not get to 100% of quota, they would simply hold sales till the next commission period – now that's a fatal flaw.

What's a fatal flaw again? Any design that has unintended bad consequences. For example, keeping this simple, I have seen sales comp designs that pay $5,000 for 99% of quota and then $10,000 for 100% of quota. This sounds nice – a big kicker to get to quota. However, what really happens in this situation? The company pays $5,000 in commissions for $1 of incremental revenue – crazy and makes no sense.

Many fatal flaws are addressed in detail in this book. For now, recognize that there are frequently used sales comp design ideas that create terrible unintended consequences. See the first page of this book, if you are experiencing any of these, you may have some fatal flaws in your designs.

Another way to think about fatal flaws in sales comp designs is that there are probably numerous sales comp designs that will work for an organization. There are no perfect designs. However, sales comp plans with fatal flaws in them will kill a sales organizations performance. Think of it this way; if you have any fatal flaws in a sales comp design, you cannot have Sales Comp Made Easy nor a successful company.

Understand the design metrics you implement to avoid any fatal flaws.

Fatal Flaws in a sales comp plan wreck havoc on everything – not just the sales force!

The Five Simple, Key Steps to a Successful Sales Compensation Plan

Chapter 5 - Step 4 - Sales Comp can't do Everything – Don't even try!

I believe the first line sales manager has one of the most critical positions in a company – especially in a small company. Finding talent, understanding that talent, helping that talent succeed, deciding who to terminate, etc. are all very difficult things to do well. And yet if they are not done well, your company will never succeed!

Think back in your own experience to when you had an underperforming rep. Sometimes when you have changed a rep, all of a sudden the customers loved your company, they began buying your products, the new rep became a hero and won contests, etc. Was it the result of the new rep? Yes. However, if the first line sales manager had not found that talent, you would never have known all those customers could love you!

Focus the sales comp plan on a few key metrics. Don't try to design a plan for every rep, selling situation, individuals or even every marketing or finance objective.

Don't even use the sales comp design as the main vehicle to drive out poor performers by having your bottom performers not make any money. Have sales management drive out the poor performers – its part of their job – not the sales comp design. Weeding out poor performers is not an easy task for sales managers but your best managers, the ones you want to keep, can do it. (See my baseball analogy in the Downside Risk section later in this book.)

Sales management especially should do those things that need to be done but don't make any sense to put in the sales comp design.

Remember Sales Comp can't do Everything. Keep it simple - KISS. It's the only way to have Sales Comp Made Easy!

The Five Simple, Key Steps to a Successful Sales Compensation Plan

Chapter 6 - Step 5 - Involve Your Sales Managers and a Sales Comp Expert in the Design Process

For years *MT. OLYMPUS* selected first line sales managers (different managers each year) who, in collaboration with a sales comp design expert, developed recommendations for the sales reps, and even the sales managers themselves. The sales comp plan design development process was used as a learning experience for the first line managers and helped each participant think more strategically about their own business.

The results – Each year's recommendations were accepted by management, commissions as a percent of revenue declined dramatically over time, target pay was kept constant, and sales performance was excellent every year.

MT. WHITNEY acquired a new technology that could immediately be sold after building a new sales organization. All sales managers and reps were new. In order to develop an appropriate sales comp design, all the sales managers met for two days with a sales comp expert.

Several hours into the meeting, as different approaches were being evaluated, one sales manager stood up and commented about one proposal, and "I don't like communistic sales comp designs." There was a senior sales VP in the room who wanted to shut down the disrespectful feedback. No! What you want in a discussion about sales comp designs is to have openness and honesty in order to extract from the people *in the company* the right design ideas. Remember; the best ideas come from within a company not from external sources.

After the communistic comment, the following great exchange happened:

As everyone was new to each other in the meeting, the sales comp expert needed to find out why the sales manager had the perspective he did.

Question - What company did you work for before you came here?
Sales manager – Named a very large multinational company.

Question – What market share did you have at your prior company?

Sales manager -- 50% share.

Question – What share do we have here?

Sales manager – Zero.

Question – Don't you think a sales comp plan should be designed differently for one company with 50% share and a different company in the same industry that has 0% share?

Sales manager – Yes – I suppose.

Post mortem – The sales manager, now having an improved understanding of the strategic issues of a business with zero share and revenue vs. 50% share and hundreds of millions of revenue, helped design a program that lasted for four years, worked for both *MT. WHITNEY* and the sales force. The sales force grew from 0 to 50 reps and revenue increased from $0 - $50M.

I share the above discussion because it reinforces one of my key principles of Sales Comp Made Easy – many of the best design ideas come from within a company – not from any outside person or entity.

Without someone involved who understand sales comp, what can happen?

Many sales managers at *Mt. Washington* were complaining that the sales rep comp design did not cover enough of the elements that should be in the sales rep sales comp design. (The managers' real problem was that their manager sales comp design had elements in it that were not in their reps designs.) Therefore, they wanted to not only add the elements that were in their manager design but also other elements to help the managers do their job of managing the sales reps. Essentially they wanted more leverage over their reps from within the sales comp design – but, sales comp should not be used for things that a sales manager should be doing.

In order to demonstrate that the company was listening to the sales managers, five managers met for a two-day meeting to discuss what changes should be made in the rep design. The first morning was spent listening to how they wanted to change the design and collectively they wanted to add about 30 additional items! That's crazy! But now they could at least see one dilemma – not all sales managers thought alike. They individually thought each of their own ideas was the only idea that should be added. When they saw a potential 30 new items, they decided that was crazy. They were asked then to eliminate those they didn't need and ended up with five elements!

Reiterating - involve your sales managers in the design process. I have found this approach to be very successful, the designs don't break the companies "bank," reps and managers are motivated and even the marketing and finance organizations have liked the results.

A side benefit of this approach is that the sales managers will then "own" the design and be more willing to enthusiastically communicate the design to their reps.

Sales comp design is a critical element of a company's success – remember *EVEREST* in chapter 1! Yes, there are many important inputs into sales comp design (sales, marketing, finance, HR, legal, etc.) but the *process* should not just be a 1 – 2 day multidisciplinary committee meeting. Apply the necessary resources, time to get the design right and involve your first line sales managers – this process will bring a huge benefit to your company.

The design leader should be the sales comp expert. Also, one person should own the process. That individual should obtain input from all the appropriate areas that need to provide input. Then there should be individual and group meetings closing with a 1 – 3 day committee meeting to finalize the design recommendations. (Sales rep designs may be able to be completed in 2 days but if sales manager designs are to be developed as well, 3 days may work best. The design meeting itself can be a multidisciplinary group (Sales, Finance, Marketing, HR, etc.) but my experience has been that sales managers themselves with the right leadership by someone who understands sales comp will develop the best designs. The final design coming from a sales manager team in combo with a sales comp expert will be reviewed by all the necessary parties anyway so why not let them take the first stab at it?

Why just sales managers? I get more candor and better designs if the participants are all sales managers at the same level in an organization. Don't have a committee of VP's, Directors and managers. Corporate America being what it is, employees won't share as openly or honestly what they really think if their boss or other corporate leaders are part of the meeting. Use the first lines sales managers only. As long as the committee and company know that just a recommendation is being developed - not necessarily the final design – why should the other functions care if sales managers design the initial draft?

If the leader of the design meeting is knowledgeable about sales comp, the company's goals, challenges the thinking of the committee, and asks tons of thought-provoking questions to get the right ideas out of the company itself, the final design should work quite well and not have any fatal flaws in it.

Somewhere late in the design approval process, the rep/manager designs should be shared with a couple of trusted reps/managers to see if there are any obvious design flaws.

I have used this approach numerous times and, bottom line, companies and the sales forces liked and implemented the recommended designs.

After obtaining all the strategic/high level input, involve your sales managers and sales comp expert in the sales rep and manager design process and you will be well on your way to SCME!

p.s. I have designed numerous sales comp programs with multidisciplinary teams that have worked, but frankly my experience has been that first obtaining strategic/high level input then using a group of sales managers and a sales comp expert is the best approach.

Additional Recommendations Beyond the 5 Simple Key Steps

Chapter 7 - Time Period to Measure Performance (Months, Quarters, or Years)

Simply, I believe quarterly sales comp designs work best. They give reps time to plan and implement the plan, recover from a shortfall, contact more customers, etc. Quarterly plans need, however, to deliver reasonable monthly cash and that can be done. There are places for monthly sales comp designs and annual plans but for the majority of business to business long term relationship driven sales processes, I think quarterly plans work best.

Think about a month. It's only 20 days long. Wow, that's short to try to have a design that strategically drives behavior. How many customers do your reps have? Can they call on all of them in a month, much less build better relationships with them in a month? Months come and go so quickly. No time for planning. Also, twelve commission periods a year give your reps twelve times during the year to think about "Can I make my plan this month? If not, I'll just hold some sales till next month when my payout rate may be higher." Twelve times they get to think this way. "Which month should I put my sales into?"

Also, monthly designs make it difficult to have a well-rounded overall compensation strategy because you have to deliver 100% of commission earnings every month.

Annual plans don't work either. Possible attainment of quota and receiving the commensurate rewards are so far in the future that there is more fear and uncertainty developed in the sales force then greed. You want greed. You want the sales reps thinking they can get to and over quota and make money frequently during the year – quarterly – but not too frequently – monthly – quarterly yields a balanced time period.

A modified YTD design measures performance and pays commissions on a YTD basis. This design fails the same way the annual plan does. At some time during the year, underperforming reps will realize they can't achieve their quota for the year. What will they do?

Some, very few, will continue beating their heads on the wall and keep trying but most will become demoralized, mentally quit, or actually quit. If they stay they will complain about everything; their quota, prices, products, everything is bad, bad, bad.

Quarterly plans aren't perfect either, but they are much better then monthly or annual or YTD plans. They have enough time for you to build some strategy into your sales comp designs. Also, employees have enough time to recover from failed sales calls and make additional calls.

One of the key issues in quarterly sales comp designs is how to deliver monthly cash without the risk of sales people owing the company money at the end of a quarter. There are numerous ways to deliver monthly cash without risk of overpaying but however you do it, keep it simple. The real measure of how a rep is performing with a quarterly sales comp design is how they did for the quarter, not any one month.

Since we are talking about quarters, quarterize everything. Have everything to do with the sales force begin and end with your quarters; new hire guarantee's, realignments, contests, promotions, everything.

Try quarterly measures – you'll find you'll like them.

Additional Recommendations Beyond the 5 Simple Key Steps

Chapter 8 - How to Have One Sales Comp Design When You Have Large Differences in Territory Volumes

At *Eagle Mountain,* annual territory base revenue ranged from $170,000 to $950,000. A large range and I have seen much larger but for now I'll just focus on *Eagle Mountain.* The sales comp design we built at *Eagle Mountain* used a *volume independent design for performance from 0% – 70% of quota. For performance between 70% and 100% of quota a flat percent of revenue was used. Over quota, two tiers were implemented that had successively higher payout rates as performance improved.

A volume independent design means that regardless of territory size, all reps make the same money for the same performance. Using Eagle mountain as an example, if two reps had different sized territories but performed at 55% (<70%) they each made the same commission. If two different sized territories performed at 69%, they each made the same commission.

One objective of the *Eagle Mountain* design was to have the range of "at quota" commissions be relatively narrow. We ended up with a range of $25,000 between the smallest volume territory and the largest volume territory for "at quota" performance.

At other companies with large variations in territory sizes, I have used similar designs but different payout rates or even different programs but I don't like these approaches. They result in too many issues to constantly juggle.

One constant I use in most companies' designs, for all territories regardless of size – has been to use the same payout rate structure for over quota performance. As long as you don't use % of over quota performance in your sales comp calculations - which you should never do - all reps can have the same design over quota.

Try to have one comp design for your entire sales force – it will help make it a Sales Comp Plan Made Easy plan.

Additional Recommendations Beyond the 5 Simple Key Steps

Chapter 9 - Range of Rep at Plan Compensation

MT. KENYA's reps had a wide range of territory volume (from $300,000 - $2,500,000). The two largest reps accounted for 1/3rd of the company's total revenue. Since *MT. KENYA's* sales comp design was *volume dependent, the two largest volume reps were very highly paid and accounted for a disproportionate percentage of the total compensation budget.

Volume Dependent Design – Example: A rep is simply paid 5% of all sales. Think Real Estate sales.

MT. KENYA wanted to redesign sales comp but anything they did which kept everyone whole meant they did not have enough money to hire the next group of reps.

The problem began with having a volume *dependent* sales comp design in the first place.

How to get out of this dilemma and not lose the two large reps? Talk to them!

They came to the company for the same reason almost everyone else did. It was a start up and the two large reps wanted to make a killing due to lucrative over quota rates and equity sales in an IPO or sale of the company.

In order to have a manageable commission budget for the next few years, a quota dependent model was implemented and the two high volume reps were granted stock options because their "at quota" compensation was reduced. The stock options had a vesting schedule that retained the two largest reps. Bottom line, no one left and *MT. KENYA* liked the design enough to use a similar concept for OUS operations.

Post Mortem, if *MT. KENYA* had had the appropriate design in the first place, this issue never would have happened and the stock options could have been given to someone else. Another example of how fatal flaws can have huge unintended bad consequences for a company.

The following true story I have seen so many times that I won't use a mountain name to identify the company but rather a mountain range – the Rockies' - which contain many individual mountains. ☺☺☺

The *ROCKY'S* rep and manager payout rates and quota's were adjusted every month based on the performance in the prior month. (I have also seen the same thing done on a quarterly basis.) In order to keep "at quota" commissions constant between reps, for those reps and managers who had the most growth, their payout rate for revenue in the subsequent time period declined the most. Your best reps look at this as "Because they performed well, their potential commissions are being reduced." You do not want your best reps thinking this way!

Following is what happened to two sales reps in *ROCKY'S* sales force. The reps each had a revenue quota of $1,000,000 and they had a payout rate of 10% of revenue at 100% of quota. Therefore, at 100% of quota, each rep earned $100,000. ($1,000,000 X's 10% = $100,000) In month one, Rep A achieved 120% of quota or $1,200,000. Rep B achieved 80% of quota or $800,000. For the subsequent time period, *in order to have both reps have the same "target pay" at 100% performance to their quota*, Rep A was given a payout rate of 8.33% ($1,200,000 X 8.33% - $100,000) and Rep B was given a payout rate of 12.5%. ($800,000 X 12.5% = $100,000)

Notice the best performing rep in this simple illustration now had the lower payout rate on revenue, "I'm good so I got penalized..." Not how you want your best reps thinking. Yes, it must be this way if you want to keep targeted pay within a certain range. However, if the sales comp design was **not** based on different payout rates for different sized territories but rather was based on a quota based target, it would be much easier to sell that design, especially to your best reps. (Example - For 100% performance, every rep makes $10,000.) Administration of the plan would also be incredibly much simpler – Sales Comp Made Easy.

For a growing company, especially a fast growing company, use a design that keeps all your reps compensation "at 100% of quota" the same (or as close together as possible), regardless of territory size. (I'm not talking about some industries like real estate or insurance.)

If you keep compensation for 100% of quota the same or similar for all reps, it's much easier and less costly to continue to add reps and managers to your sales force. Once you start allowing volume to dictate differences in compensation at 100% of quota, it becomes more difficult and expensive to split territories, add reps and, revise the strategic direction of the sales comp design.

In the very early stages of a company's development when you may have no clue on what to expect in performance, you may need a design that is volume dependent allowing reps to make huge sums of money but also growing the company very fast. There's nothing wrong with this! Just make sure the payout rates don't destroy your margins. Also, communicate to your sales force that the sales comp design will periodically change but for exceptional performance they will continue to be able to earn significant income – regardless of the design. Also, if equity is being offered in any form, reinforce the potential long term value of that as well.

Range of rep at plan compensation – the narrower the better for as long as you can.

Additional Recommendations Beyond the 5 Simple Key Steps

Chapter 10 - Upside Opportunity

When should you hold down potential upside income? When you have no clue what quotas should be and you run the risk of your sales people leaving for competition or somewhere else if their incomes fall off the table.

Prior to DRGs being implemented in the 1980's, companies and the entire medical community were uncertain about what would happen to prices, procedures, volumes, etc. once DRG's were implemented. (More recently, think of what happened when Bill Clinton became President and most medical companies lost significant market value in the first six months of his Presidency.)

Recognizing the uncertainty DRG's would bring, *MT. BAKER* implemented a sales comp design where upside potential was reduced but this was also offset with less risk below plan. *MT. BAKER* was afraid they wouldn't know if a rep was over quota as the result of good performance or the result of the quota being too low. Same for below quota performance. Was that going to be because the quota was set to high or was it because the rep was a poor performer?

The new design worked. I'll call the design more conservative – less risk and less reward near quota then the previous design. Reps stayed, they earned reasonable incomes, and when more certainty developed in the marketplace over the mega issue related to DRG implementation, income potential over quota was increased and more risk was put back in the sales comp plan below quota.

This was a great example of strategic macro environmental issues impacting sales comp design for several years. The first year bringing less risk to both sales people and *MT. BAKER* and in a subsequent year, more normal risk and reward in the sales comp design for reps and *MT. BAKER*.

To communicate the "break the bank" potential of a new sales comp design for *ELDORADO* as part of the communication process, during the national conference call announcing the new sales comp design, I broke a glass jar full of coins on top of a metal desk so it sounded like a piggy bank was breaking - which it was - but also I wanted to communicate the incredible potential in the new design. Bottom line, with the right design you want every rep breaking the bank, you want as much upside potential as possible and don't forget, have some fun too!

Have reasonable upside opportunity and communicate that potential to the sales force. You want the reps/managers to know how to break the bank and you want as many of them as possible to do exactly that.

What is reasonable up side opportunity? First, no caps on pay. By design and analysis, estimate where your very top performers may perform and allow them to earn 2 – 3 times what compensation is at 100% of quota. For example, if at quota compensation for a sales rep is $100,000 per year, allow your top performers to earn $200,000 - $300,000+.

If you have no clue how much a rep can sell over quota you don't have to worry about what they will earn if your design is right, meaning you know for ALL levels of performance what commissions as a percent of revenue will be.

Have as much upside potential as possible – push the envelope on this!

Additional Recommendations Beyond the 5 Simple Key Steps

Chapter 11 - Downside risk

GRIZZLY PEAK was adjusting its quotas, commission designs and account assignments almost every month. Crazy! All of the changes were done not on the basis of customer relationships but rather to try to manage sales rep compensation. Ridiculous!

Fast growing companies need to do things differently than a stable or mature business but one of those differences doesn't need to be realigned territories and redesigned sales comp every month.

GRIZZLY PEAK changed from a **volume dependent design to a volume independent (quota dependent) design.** For an entire year, *GRIZZLY PEAK* was able to maintain stable territories, keep the same sales comp design, and had no compensation "band-aids" while in the prior 12 months, there had been many commission band-aids, quota adjustments, etc. A major improvement from where *GRIZZLY PEAK* had been.

One CFO told me they spent more time on sales comp for the past three years then they had on any other activity – the CFO! They needed and implemented a Sales Comp Made Easy plan. The CFO went on to spend their time on more appropriate things like raising capital for the company.

Have some income protection on the down side. I didn't say a lot, I said some. A simple comparison to baseball Hall of Famers may help here. Baseball Hall of Famers did not have Hall of Fame years *every* year of their career. They had ups and downs, just like your sales people. The same people don't *always* win every contest. The winners change.

I am not saying that you won't have reps or managers who consistently rank near the top of your sales force. You should have some sales people who do well year after year but they won't be the TOP performer every year.

If your designs have income falling off the table at too early a point in your performance curve, some of your best people are going to experience this drastic performance and income decline and then leave or you will give them band-aids. Band-aids are always a mess.

How much to band-aid?

When to band-aid?

Whom to band-aid?

Criteria for the band-aid?

Etc.

Will any band-aid criteria be applied consistently? Probably not.

Sales comp band-aids of any form, especially if you have lots of them, are a sign of a poorly designed plan.

Have downside risk but if you're doing a lot of "band-aids", you should build some of the income protection you are giving away anyway in the band aids - right in the design.

Additional Recommendations Beyond the 5 Simple Key Steps

Chapter 12 - Split credits

Think of the last fight you had with someone, maybe your spouse. Who was at fault *and*, to what *degree*? You really don't know do you? Neither will you ever know who should get how much of a split sale.

Try to avoid split credits but if you have to allocate sales between two or more people, split the credit evenly and be consistent about the split. Next time the value brought by each person will change anyway and, never forget, KISS.

Don't try to scientifically determine how to split credits – do it evenly because you simply can't figure out what the right split should be anyway and, on each sale, each person's value will be different.

Additional Recommendations Beyond the 5 Simple Key Steps

Chapter 13 - Compensation for territory splits

TWIN SISTERS analyzed reps performance over several years with an effort to determine "Who was most likely to win the annual rep contest." Many criteria were evaluated including tenure, age, volume, technical or sales background, performance review category, market share, when/if they had had their territory split, and many others. The single most *predictive* event of who would be in the running for the next years "Rep of the year type awards" were those reps *that had most recently had their territory split.* The winners included both the "old" reps as well as new hires. Amazing.

At the time of a reps *fifth* career split, two reps had been hired to take over customers being "given up" in the new territory realignment. In a sales meeting where the split was being discussed, the new reps became concerned about how their hiring would impact the income and their future relationship with the incumbent rep. "Don't worry about me," the incumbent rep said, "I have been split four times before and my income post split has gone up every time." The rep's income went up not because the territory realignment boost compensations was so lucrative, it wasn't. The reps income went up because the rep was an outstanding rep who whenever he could focus more on new business, he would get that new business. Also, he had a territory split boost program that made sense because it was built with the dynamics of that business and the company's economics in mind!

Bottom line, the best reps are the ones that generally get split. They get a smaller number of customers to focus on, spend less time in maintenance activities and go grow their business again and again and again!

For a fast growing business where you expect significant rep headcount growth, with an appropriate sales comp design and territory split boost program, territory splits can be accomplished with minimal pain to the company and reps.

For a company that is growing rapidly, you need to have the capability of adding reps without a huge disruption in *morale and income* if you are to grow at anywhere near the rate you could grow at! Also, these fast growing companies will constantly be adding reps and splitting territories. It's just the way it is and your sales force needs to understand this.

At the same time, you need to protect the income of the reps/managers being split and protect the company from spending too much money on territory realignment payments.

If you are growing fast, you should have part or all of your design based on what I call a "volume independent" design. As mentioned at the beginning in the definitions section, a "volume independent" design means that regardless of the size of a territory, all reps earn the same or similar compensation at 100% of quota. For example, at 100% of quota, all reps earn $10,000, or close to it, in commissions. This approach completely solves the territory split compensation issue because when a rep has their territory split, they don't experience a decrease in compensation at 100% of quota.

Territory split boost programs can be built that are economical for the company and yet motivational for the sales force. Reps need income protection for a period of time after a split and the company needs to provide this in as inexpensive a manner as possible. If you use a territory split boost program, it should be built based on the expected growth rate for the company and should be designed in such a way that the reps that are split still have risk in their compensation based on their performance. The boost compensation should simply be a payment added onto whatever else the rep earns – over or under quota.

One of the factors to consider as you build your sales comp design is your anticipated future growth. The core design will then more likely last for several years, commissions as a percent of revenue will decrease over time (increased leverage to finance folks) and be easier to change if necessary every year.

Managing sales reps income and company costs for territory splits are key factors in having Sales Comp Made Easy - especially for fast growing companies.

Additional Recommendations Beyond the 5 Simple Key Steps

Chapter 14 - What % of Reps Should Achieve or Exceed Quota?

Assuming national performance around 100% of quota, 60% - 70% of your reps should achieve quota. Why? Simply it works.

Targeting 80% - 90% of your reps to be at or above 100% of quota drives quotas too low. Targeting 40% - 50% or less of your reps to be at or above 100% of quota means the quotas are too high and many reps and managers will become discouraged.

Fundamentally, sales people want to achieve their quotas.

If you target this metric at all, target 60% - 70% of reps achieving their quotas when the nation is performing at plan.

Additional Recommendations Beyond the 5 Simple Key Steps

Chapter 15 - Recommended Design Process

I have successfully used the following design process numerous times to develop sales comp plans (and contests) that the major interested parties (finance, marketing, HR and the sales force itself) all found to be acceptable.

The focus of the process is *design* but if you use sales managers, note that it will always be tough to get their minds off *level of pay.* However, it can be done!

Prior to any meetings, become knowledgeable of all the key perspectives from – executives, sales, marketing, finance, HR. (market pay, quota development process, company strategy, products, prices, strategic direction, etc.)

Have a few conference calls and or meetings then have a design meeting. The design meeting (which may take several days) agenda should include the following.

1. A short educational section on how and how not to design sales comp plans. This gives the audience a common platform on which to evaluate different approaches. Also, as part of the education piece, especially if the audience is all sales managers, it should be clearly communicated that the purpose of the committee *is not level of pay but design.* At times this has been quite difficult for sales managers to grasp and get them away from level of pay but simply - you just need to do that. If you can't get the sales managers off from the level of pay topic, here's one thing I have done. Numerous times when I was having difficulty getting sales managers off the topic of level of pay, I have simply said – "Fine. At plan pay currently is $100,000/year. As of this moment we have increased at plan pay to $200,000. We will use $200,000 as the pay target for this meeting and then at the end, we will just cut everything we recommend in half." This approach finally got the sales managers off pay level and onto design where they needed to be.
2. Determine the pay level of the jobs being discussed.

3. Decide what the mix of salary and commissions should be at 100% of quota.
4. Decide on what the range of "at quota" compensation should be.
5. Make sure everyone has the same information on the unique dynamics of the company's products, sales tactics, marketing plans, anticipated future growth, headcount adds/deletions, range of territory volumes, growth vs. last year, etc.
6. Decide on what the commission elements should be. What do you want to pay for?
7. What should be the weight of each element in the commission plan?
8. For each element, what should be the ramp rates above and below quota?

After the recommendations are developed, they have to be modeled for cost purposes and communication materials need to be developed.

The communication materials should start with the objectives of the sales comp design, the process and team members that were on the design committee, and the design itself. If a Sales Comp Made Easy design has been developed, the communication materials for the design should be quite brief. Collateral information like any boost program, promotion criteria, eligibility criteria, etc. should all be covered in a separate very detailed document.

The leader of this meeting(s) must understand sales comp design well enough to avoid fatal flaws, break the bank programs, etc.

A couple things about these design meetings based on actual experiences –

1. Never think you can over communicate a sales comp plan. At times, you will have some reps or managers who never quite understand the design. Do your best to help every rep understand the design. However, I have found some consistent high performers who for unknown reasons, never quite "get" any sales comp design. If they keep performing, just let them be – there's something in their nature other than a sales comp design that drives them to succeed.
2. Also, as pointed out elsewhere in this book, sales managers like to have the sales comp design do some of their work for them but don't build a design that does this. Make your sales managers

manage and let the sales comp design drive behavior and reward people, Sales Comp Made Easy.

You can never over-communicate a sales comp plan! The plan needs to be communicated originally, but then follow up needs to happen throughout the life of the compensation plan to ensure sales people still understand it. A sales force changes constantly; realignments, turnover, new products/prices, new people in general, etc.

The above design meeting agenda has worked numerous times to develop Sales Comp Made Easy plans – try it- you'll like it – it's simple!

Additional Recommendations Beyond the 5 Simple Key Steps

Chapter 16 - When Should a Sales Comp Plan be Communicated?

MAUNA KEA changed their sales comp design *every few* months and sometimes even after a commission time period was over! What went on all the time? Late every month - the prime time when you would want your sales force focused on getting sales, not calling internally in your company - reps would call finance, HR, the commission analyst, anyone close to the commission process to try to figure out what the new design would look like. If they could learn anything, it would help them decide in which time period they should book their current months sales – crazy! After this small but fast growing company implemented a design with fast growth in mind, a design lasted an entire year and even quotas – which had been a mess – were able to be communicated for six months at a time.

Sales comp plans should be communicated as soon as possible after the time period begins which applies to the new comp plan. Never before! Communicating a spiff or design before it starts will only have your sales force trying to determine which time period any current sales should fall into. You never want to do this. One company I worked with communicated all their sales comp plans and quotas on the very first day of every fiscal year. Outstanding.

If quotas are to be communicated at the same time as the sales comp design, it is fine to wait a few days into the year to communicate them as a package. Especially if part of your comp/quota system is based on the prior year; you won't know those numbers are until the year has been over for a few days.

I have seen some companies communicate the sales comp plan six months after the plan was supposed to begin. This is totally inappropriate. It's usually the result of a company fearing commissions will be too expensive but that is really not the issue. The main issue is that the company loses far more in the motivation of their sales force by not communicating the sales comp plan in a timely manner.

For Sales Comp Made Easy, communicate your designs as early as possible after you have begun the time period the design covers.

Additional Recommendations Beyond the 5 Simple Key Steps

Chapter 17 - Who and How Should the Sales Comp Plans be Communicated?

How should the sales comp plans be communicated? – As simply as possible. To communicate how simple *ACONCAGUA*'s sales comp design was going to be, sales managers were instructed to tear an 8.5 X 11 piece of paper into a piece of paper that was about 2 inches by 2 inches. *ACONCAGUA* had two product lines so each side of the paper was used to communicate the design for one product line. The sales managers were instructed to use the tiny piece of paper to communicate the design as a way of demonstrating to their sales reps that the sales comp design was quite simple. This was a great approach for an organization that had been continually griping about design complexity.

The design team with a sales management leader should communicate the design to all first line sales managers. Once the first line sales managers understand the rep and their own programs, they should then communicate the sales comp plan to their teams. There should be a group call/meeting as well as follow up individual calls.

Not only should the sales comp design team "own" and communicate the design, you want all first line sales managers to "own" and communicate the design to their own respective reps as well. If sales managers know they or their peers had significant input into the designs, they will not have the attitude that corporate, HR, finance, "some else" designed the plan. This will diminish or eliminate sales managers making comments to their reps like - "That's why it's bad – we had no input into it. Corporate designed it, Finance did it, etc."

The design team and a senior sales leader should communicate the new sales comp design. It is helpful to also have comp calculators and quotas available to reps.

Additional Recommendations Beyond the 5 Simple Key Steps

Chapter 18 - Who Should a Sales Comp Plan "Work For"?

The sales comp plan should first of all for the ... company! The design must be aligned with the objectives of the company. The company must be able to afford the investment in the sales force.

Also, if the design works for about 80% of the sales reps, it's a good design. A design can't be developed that works for 100% of your reps. Don't even try, it won't work.

I'm not trying to be political here but think about it this way. What country in the world has the most successful economy? Which country has the largest middle class? Does the economy work for everyone in that country? No. Does the country have rich, poor, and a significant middle class. Yes. Same for your sales comp plan. If your sales comp plan works for the majority of your reps, the middle class, it's a good plan and you are well on your way to a Sales Comp Made Easy plan.

As mentioned elsewhere, don't try to starve out poor performers. Yes, have commission risk in the designs but also provide some income support for individuals below quota. Even your best performers will have bad quarters or years. If the design is the biggest or sole approach to pushing reps out of your organization because they don't make any money, some of your best people will eventually be caught in this and leave.

Who should a compensation plan "work" for? The company first and about 80% of your sales force.

Fatal Flaws

Chapter 19 - Fatal Flaw - Linked Incentives

A rep must meet one performance metric to earn a bonus in another category.

Simply - avoid these.

MAUNA LOA had two main products sold to two different types of physicians. However, the sales comp design used a grid concept where in order to make much money, a rep or manager had to perform exceptionally well in *both* products. Yes, the company saved a ton of commission dollars but performance (revenue growth) was a disaster! No one liked the design other than the finance folks. If the reps won in one product, they wanted to win in their commissions but it didn't work that way. You had to be perfect but nobody was or ever will be perfect!

The sales comp plan was redesigned to allow *winning* in commissions if a rep was successful with even only one product. Morale improved as well as results – in both product lines!

If you must have linked incentives, make the thresholds for the links as easy to achieve as possible. Then, if you have made them easy to achieve, you have to ask yourself why have them at all? Just like thresholds, linked incentives are sometimes a crutch for sales management – abdicating their job of getting the sales force to do their jobs – selling everything. Linked incentives may look nice on the surface but they don't work as well as they look. They are too confusing for reps to understand and drive their behavior. KISS – avoid linked incentives.

If you simply MUST have some links, approach the links like this:
Achieve any 2 of 5 metrics to get "X" vs. achieve all five metrics
Achieve any 3 of 5 metrics at a 70% performance level vs. 100%
Note – Both of the above at least have some appearance of achievability.

Fatal Flaw – Linked incentives.

Chapter 20 - Fatal Flaw - Believing Your Reps have Accurate Quotas

CARLTON PEAK adjusted quotas every quarter based on what the rep did in the prior quarter. Therefore the best performing reps continually had the most difficult quotas to achieve. Just the opposite of what you want – feeding the turkeys and starving the eagles. There had to be a better way and in fact, using Sales Comp Made Easy, we implemented a new quota growth approach requiring all territories to have minimum growth amounts and additional growth was required based on the unique dynamics of the company and industry.

Following is the first and *exact* quote from the sales force after having had in the past continually changing sales comp designs and terrible quota development:

"... I just wanted to let you know how impressed I was with today's call and the thoughtfulness you put into the 20XX comp plan. The motivators, fairness, and opportunity to excel are clearly laid out in the plan. I can really see the hard work and thought you put into it and am looking forward to working hard to exceed plan and bringing our products to those customers who need them..."

Sales Comp Made Easy includes good quota development as well!

Surprise, most likely your monthly/quarterly unit/revenue quotas are not as accurate as you think and here's why:

Consider the process. A national quota is developed that is a compromise between different perspectives (sales, marketing, finance, senior management). Since it's a compromise of different perspectives, by default it can't be perfect. The national annual quota may be reasonable but then the national annual quota is split into quarters and months and then each quarter and month is split into areas, regions, districts, territories. Wow. And a rep's monthly and quarterly quotas are supposed to be perfect? No way!

The territory/rep level month or quarterly quotas simply can't be accurate after being pulled through this entire guessing game process. Even though the quotas won't be accurate, you still need to give sales people quotas but remember, by default they won't be anywhere near perfect.

More established businesses will have more accurate quotas and as accuracy improves slightly, you can add more risk and reward to the sales comp design.

Fatal Flaw – Thinking your quotas, especially monthly or quarterly territory level quotas, are accurate – they simply aren't.

Fatal Flaws

Chapter 21 - Fatal Flaw – Too many elements and/or Design Complexity

A sales comp plan can be quite simple. Reference chapter 17 for a billion dollar business sales comp plan communicated via a 2 X 2 piece of paper – simple!

The design worked partly because it was obviously quite simple. Sales Comp Made Easy!

Yes, I brought the KISS principle in the key 5 steps. However, this issue of complexity or, to many elements in a plan occurs so frequently that it deserves another chapter.

If your design has five or more elements, your sales force doesn't know what you want them to do. Four elements are a lot but may be OK. Three elements, now you have focus and a simple design that is more likely to be effective.

One or two elements are even better. Simple and clear direction. Have your sales management team get all the rest of the stuff you want or need done through their management expertise or find some new managers.

Fatal Flaw – Complexity or too many soles compensation design elements. KISS. Have as few metrics as possible and let sales management get the other things done that need doing. Sales Comp Made Easy.

Chapter 22 - Fatal Flaw - Step or Flat Areas in your Payout Rates

GRANITE PEAK analyzed the results of several of their divisions that had step or flat rates in their commission designs. The statistics were amazing about where reps performed. Rarely did reps perform just under any break point. They almost *always* performed just over the breakpoints, meaning that if they could not get to the next higher payout level, they had held back sales in one time period with their intent being that they might earn a higher payout rate in the next commission period.

MAMMOUTH MOUNTAIN had a step rate where for going from 99.49% of plan to 99.50% of plan (about $500) the reps commissions increased by $4,000! It didn't make any sense! The design was changed and eliminated the crazy flat rate.

Reiterating - Flat parts in your payout rates don't make sense. For example, a rep makes $5,000 at 99% of plan and $10,000 at 100% of plan. Essentially, for $1 of additional revenue, the rep earns $5,000 in commissions. Does this make sense? No. And yet I have seen this logic in many sales comp designs. It simply doesn't make sense.

The same thing happens whenever you have "steps" in your payout rates, not just around 100% of plan. Wherever you have step payout rates in your designs, if a rep can't get to the next breakpoint of higher rates, they will hold back to try and get into the higher payout tier the next time period. At least, I would. Maximizing sales comp for a rep made easy – not a good idea. This doesn't make sense. Don't make it too easy for them!

Let sales employees earn more commissions on a continuum basis. Besides, it's a much simpler design as well because you don't have to guess how many reps will earn the lump bonuses and how frequently that will happen. Sales Comp Made Easy.

Fatal Flaw – Avoid step or flat areas in your payout schedules. They look attractive and they are, but really only for your reps. The step and or flat rates allow your reps to maximize their incomes without maximizing their performance which is not a good idea.

Fatal Flaws

Chapter 23 - Fatal Flaw - Thresholds (Example: "You must achieve 80% of quota prior to earning any commissions.")

MT. SHASTA released a brand new, game changing and share grabbing technology. The product was launched around the world at the same time. One geography decided that since the technology was so different, incredible, and unique that they would redesign their sales comp plan to pay more money over plan and those incremental commission "costs" would be saved by implementing a very high threshold of performance before any commissions would be paid. Seems reasonable – a new dynamic product – every rep should easily be near or over quota – right? Wrong!

Every geography had great success with the new product other then the geography that established an unusually high threshold in their sales comp design. If the threshold was not met, no commissions were paid.

What happened in the high threshold geography while the rest of the world had stellar performance?

Reps were waking up every morning spending more time and energy wondering if they would ever get to the threshold then being positive and out with customers sharing the great product news.

During the first half of the year, performance in the high threshold geography was far below expectations as well as far below the performance of other geographies around the world. Effective with the 2nd half of the year, the threshold was eliminated. No other changes were made in the sales comp design, prices, quotas, or people. The only thing that changed was the elimination of the threshold. Performance in the second half of the year was outstanding and comparable to the performance of other geographies around the world. It's crazy that such a small thing as a sales comp threshold could impact a geography's performance – but it did!

The *KILAMANJARO* CEO thought reps should not get paid unless they achieved their quota. After all, quota was the reps *job*. For the first year, the CEO continually had issues with their sales force not having thresholds. The CEO wanted thresholds in the design but they weren't there. Many conversations and meetings were held around this topic. However, as the CEO watched his sales force consistently meet and exceed their quotas and goals, be happy, hungry, and enthusiastic, the CEO finally relented and no longer promoted the concept of having thresholds. Sales Comp Made Easy!

I hate thresholds. If you must have thresholds, make the threshold as easy to achieve as possible. Companies put thresholds in because they think they may save some commission dollars for those reps that perform below the threshold. The reality is that the companies actually lose revenue as reps that cannot get to some artificial threshold will hold revenue until the next period when they may make the threshold. You never want a sales comp design that has elements in it that encourage a rep to hold sales. Ever!

Also, I think part of the reason companies have thresholds – other than to try to save some commission dollars on the poorest of the poor performers, is like "linked incentives," where sales management is trying to use the sales comp design to do things that sales management should do. Simply managing poor performers either out of the organization or helping them improve their results! If someone is not performing, sales management should help them, get them the right tools to do their job or put them on a performance improvement plan or move them out. Don't wait for a threshold to keep kicking in, with the rep then not earning any money and finally leaving the organization. Sales management step up. Do your job!

Think about your own company. Do you have thresholds? If you do, what do you do when one of your stars falls below the threshold? Do you *ever do fixes, adjustments, quota changes, etc.?* If you do these things or you would do these things for a star or two be honest with yourself, your thresholds are either too high or because of the adjustments, you really don't have thresholds. If you do adjustments or are willing to lower the threshold to a more easily achieved level, why have them at all?

I think companies with aggressive thresholds are missing the boat. For the few dollars they may be saving in commissions they are potentially losing thousands/millions? of dollars in revenue because if a rep can't get to a threshold, what are they going to do? Wait until the next commission period to put in any sales they can defer.

Finally, thresholds just generate questions that are difficult to answer. For example; Where to set the threshold? Same or different than last year? Different for different territories or since quotas are not perfect should there be different thresholds for different products or ???

Fatal Flaw – Thresholds. Eliminate them or if you must have them make them as easy to achieve as possible and then ask yourself – do you really need them? Probably not.

Fatal Flaws

Chapter 24 - Fatal Flaw – Year-end Large Bonus Payments

At *WHITE MOUNTAIN*, the light dawns on a first line sales manager. The sales manager passionately wanted to include large year-end bonus in the sales comp design to drive annual performance. After understanding what I have written below about how year-end bonuses work and really don't motivate very many reps for very long, the sales managers response was, "I guess we would never want to have year-end bonuses in our sales comp plan would we?" My answer, No.

Who is motivated by year-end bonuses? Everyone on the first day of the year? Hardly. The reward is too far in the future and it is too uncertain if the required performance will be achieved.

How about later in the year? Let's see. Let's use an example of what happens after _nine months_ into a year:

Rep A is 200% of quota YTD and almost guaranteed to exceed the bonus requirement. Is rep A motivated by the potential year-end bonus?
Probably not.
Why? They're going to get the bonus anyway.

Rep B is 50% of YTD quota and almost guaranteed not to get the bonus.
Is rep B motivated by the potential year-end bonus?
Probably not.
Why? They are too far below quota and can't get back to 100% by year end, at least that's how most reps would think. (The rep would have to – round numbers - perform at about a 300% rate to make up for all the lost ground earlier in the year.)

Rep C is at 95-105% of YTD performance.
Is rep C motivated by the potential year-end bonus?

Yes. They probably are motivated because they are "on the bubble." Maybe they will and maybe they won't get to 100% of quota.

So, if a company has placed lots of money in a year-end bonus, it will motivate only a few reps and for those few reps only for a few months of the year! It's probably a waste of whatever commission dollars are budgeted for the year-end bonus.

Far better to have rolled the end of the year bonus money into the sales comp plan during the year motivating more reps for a longer period of time.

Every company I have ever worked with who had year-end bonuses in their designs eventually eliminated them.

Fatal Flaw - Large year-end bonuses. Put the budgeted money elsewhere in your designs to maximize the motivational value of that money.

Fatal Flaws

Chapter 25 - Fatal Flaw – CAPS

Very rarely should CAP's be in a sales comp design. A good sales comp design should eliminate the need for CAP's.

There are some very rare situations when CAPS can be used - MBO's are one example.

CAPS could also be used in the following crazy example. A sales rep sells nuclear reactors. They sell one to Waco TX. The next day they sell another one to Waco TX. This doesn't make sense. There should be a CAP on selling nuclear reactors to Waco TX. They only need one. Simple.

Fatal Flaw – CAPS – don't use them.

Chapter 26 - Fatal Flaw - Unique Payout Rates and even a unique comp plan for Every Sales Rep and Manager

Ridiculous. This makes no sense.

STONE MOUNTAIN had the following sales comp designs for their sales force of *30* reps –

-Distributors – Distributors who purchased product and then resold it.

-Sales Agents – They did not buy the product but were paid "X%" of what they sold.

-Commission only employees.

-Salary and commission employees

-Salary and bonus employees.

-Salary, bonus and commission employees.

Thirty reps and 6 sales comp designs with several permutations of some of the designs as well. Crazy. Sales Comp **Not** Made Easy! They even had one design where a rep at the end of the year could (and did) owe *STONE MOUNTAIN* money. The rep literally wrote a check to *STONE MOUNTAIN* . Crazy.

Most importantly, with the multiplicity of designs, *STONE MOUNTAIN* could not get consistent implementation of their sales objectives! The sales force had too many directions to follow and the reps and managers actually all hated the difference in the designs because *everyone thought everyone else had a better deal!*

The above situation was corrected by offering employment to all non-employees (distributors and agents) including the buy-out of contracts. Then **one** simple Sales Comp Made Easy program was designed in collaboration with five sales mangers that worked. *STONE MOUNTAIN's* business had been flat for three years but after the massive sales comp redesign, *STONE MOUNTAIN* revenue began growing again in the low single digits!!

As I have stated elsewhere in this book but worth repeating here, companies sometimes take the multiple design approach because they want to deliver sales comp that is the same for all reps/managers at

100% of quota even though there is a large variation in territory size. Using a design like this requires constant recalculations of the payout rates due to territory changes but more importantly, every rep has different "ramp" rates of pay at least for performance below 100% of quota.

A much better approach is simply to use the pay target you have already established to "back into" the rates (say $10,000 for 100% performance) and then below plan, allow compensation to decrease with performance based on performance vs. quota. For over quota performance, use a commission formula that has payout rates based on the actual revenue over quota.

Over quota **do not** use % of quota for your payout rates as small territories could achieve astronomical percentages over quota and commensurately earn inappropriately high commissions.

Isosceles Peak Mountain implemented a program that used % of quota for over plan payout rates. Immediately after the first quarter checks went out, *Isosceles Peak Mountain*'s largest volume reps called the national sales VP to complain about the large checks several small territories earned as the result of having small quotas and therefore when they went over quota, they earned extraordinary %'s of quota and commensurately very high commission checks. *Isosceles Peak Mountain* had the choice of changing the design of the over quota rates or spending an extra $250,000 - $500,000 on commissions that year. They chose to spend the extra money when if they had used an appropriate design, they could have more invested that money more appropriately.

Unique payout rates for every individual or groups of individuals in a commission plan make calculations a mess and don't work, so why do it?

Fatal Flaw - Avoid sales employee having unique payout rates. A huge step towards Sales Comp Made Easy!

Other Fun Stories from the Front Lines of Sales Comp

Chapter 27 - Level of Pay

I have been involved in thousands of conversations with sales people who want to leave one company for another company or simply go to a competitor. The reps manager will almost always say the reason the rep is considering leaving is about money, i.e. the reps current compensation is less than the other new company. My experience however has been that it was rarely just about money. The vast majority of the time the rep was feeling "unloved/un-appreciated" at the current company.

Other reasons reps considered leaving were the rep was going through some short term financial difficulty; marital issues, health issues, yes some financial concerns, misunderstandings about the difference in net pay between independent reps (who paid all their own expenses) and employees who received a salary, benefits, 401K, stock, etc.

My point is that when sales reps or sales managers make a lot of noise about their compensation, don't jump to the conclusion that they are underpaid relative to what their compensation should be. Investigate, investigate, investigate! You may discover changes you need to make in lots of areas other than compensation. Changes could be necessary in compensation, yes, or benefits, equity, contest structure, or many other areas.

Other Fun Stories from the Front Lines of Sales Comp

Chapter 28 - Ethics is Number 1!

The sales process should be simple. Treat your customers well, deliver on **all** your promises, and never give up.

The same is true for sales comp. Treat your "customers" (sales people) well, pay them competitively; salary, commissions and benefits. Deliver on your promises in the sales comp documents. Never give up on encouraging your sales force to meet and exceed their quotas by giving them achievable quotas and providing all the resources they need.

Finally, don't hide or mask bad news in a sales comp design. Your sales people will eventually see through any mirrors you try to implement anyway. In fact, rather than hide anything, show your sales force exactly how to "Break the Bank" in your sales comp plan. If you have appropriate quotas and a well designed sales comp plan, you want as many sales people as possible going well over quota and earning a ton of money. Properly designed sales comp plans should not only deliver for the company but also for the sales force!

Be honest – tell your sales force everything they need to know – the Good, the Bad, and the Ugly.

Other Fun Stories from the Front Lines of Sales Comp

Chapter 30 - Sales Reps Sell Based on How Their Sales Comp Plan is Designed

In the implantable device world, you have two ways you can measure sales – when a hospital purchases a product or when a device is implanted.

ANNAPURNA got fed up with product that was loaded in one quarter and then returned at a later date without obviously having been implanted. Rather than deal with a few offending reps, sales management abdicated their role of managing the sales force and implemented a sales comp design that was based on implants. This sounded nice – all sales were truly sales because after an implant, the product obviously could not be returned. The problem occurred at the end of the very first quarter of the new design.

ANNAPURNA wanted to do what they normally did, load the sales channel, however, you can't load an implant. Big problem. To get the desired result, more sales in the first quarter, *ANNAPURA* implemented a spiff that cost the company tons of incremental commission dollars. *ANNAPURNA* had the worst quarter in its history and the sales comp plan was changed back to being based on sales after only one quarter!

Another division of *ANNAPURNA* implemented a sales comp design that was only *partially* based on implants. That design lasted not only for a year, but was expanded into other products in future years.

Moral of the story - if someone not very knowledgeable about sales comp design dictates a design that is likely to have unintended bad consequences, consider having that element being a smaller component of total sales comp at first and test to see how well it will work in action.

One of my favorite stories in this regard was *Mt. Olympus*. *Mt. Olympus* had a capital and disposables sales model. Reps were paid a modest amount for disposables and received 90% of their capital equipment commissions on **receipt** of a customer order. (Not receipt of the product.)

Care to guess what happened? You're right. Lots of capital equipment orders were taken with installs being less then sales orders. In fact some installs never happened or took months.

The sales reps did what they were paid to do; get capital equipment sales orders and don't worry installs.

Post mortem – *Mt. Olympus* had lots of what I will call "anchors" in customer's hands that were never used. Sales management tried to penalize sales reps for having these anchors and yet the sales comp plan had been designed to encourage orders not installs. The "anchors" also became "dragging anchors" where their actual presence hurt sales in the local geography. Customers talked with other likely users of the product and shared how they *weren't* using the capital equipment that they had ordered.

Moral of the story, be extremely careful about how you design your sales comp plans.

Sales reps sell based on how their compensation is designed. Make sure the design reinforces the right behaviors.

Other Fun Stories from the Front Lines of Sales Comp

Chapter 31 - Develop a Sales/Sales Comp Analyst at Your Company

In order to accurately budget and forecast commission costs, you need to have an individual with great analytical skill, the ability to communicate with sales and senior management, and a sales data base that can be analyzed any way you want. The "Lina" – (an alias) of your company needs to have a good understanding of your current business and your long range strategic plan.

Accurately estimating commission costs is a huge issue for any business as the commission budget is usually a significant part of total costs. Large businesses may invest as little as single digit percentages in total sales comp while newer smaller business will allocate anywhere from 10% to 50%+ of revenue during a company's start up phase.

For a small business, the implications of inaccurate commissions budgeting are greater than in a larger company, more likely to happen, and errors have a greater impact on their business.

If sales comp is under budgeted, you end up with a demoralized sales force because sales comp may have to be reduced to avoid burning up too much cash.

If sales comp is over budgeted, investments that could have been made in other areas of the business may not be made because the assumption was those funds were needed for sales comp.

Especially then, for smaller companies, it is crucial to have an outstanding employee who is responsible for all the analytics around sales comp.

Besides an outstanding sales comp analyst, you need commission calculation software that makes it easy to calculate commissions. Sales Comp Made Easy is also about the calculation and reporting of commissions. If you follow the principles in this book about design, the calculation and reporting of commissions will also be Made Easy! There are several commission calculation software products available but most are quite expensive.

Until you have 50+ reps, you can probably use an excel based process but beyond 50 you should consider a commission software package.

I built a custom sales comp and sales contest system for one company for only $1.5M. (4,000 employees are now paid using the system - 12 years later). The annual maintenance costs are quite reasonable. This shows custom software can be economically developed.

Find or develop a great sales comp analyst in your company.

Other Fun Stories from the Front Lines of Sales Comp

Chapter 32 - Margin vs. Revenue

DENALI had 80%+ gross margins and designed their sales comp plans around revenue. That made sense. However, they redesigned their sales manager compensation plans to have 25%+ of commissions based on margin. Insane. 80%+ gross margins and the company was focusing sales management, the only group really charged with revenue growth, to think about T and E, mileage, hotels, meals, etc. Crazy! With 80% gross margins, sales reps and sales management should be laser-focused on growing revenues. Yes, sales managers should have an expense budget and should be measured on performance to that budget but in this case, the percent of their pay allocated to margin or expense management should have been much smaller or maybe even non-existent.

After one year, the margin component was eliminated because it couldn't be calculated. (With 80% plus margins, *DENALI* had never invested the money to routinely, at a grass roots level built the systems that would be able to track in real time what their margin results were – all of their IT resources for years had been appropriately been built around tracking revenues. This was one sign that margin should never have been used in the first place.

Moral of the story, in a high margin business, focus sales managers on revenue growth and use sales management to get everything else done that needs doing via sales management direction.

You may have very strong opposition to my ideas in this chapter. If you violently disagree with me and in your industry you have discovered you must use margin as the main metric rather than revenue, go ahead. My point is only that if you can use revenue, do that. Use a margin based sales comp plan only if you absolutely have to. Then use the other principles in this book but skip this one on margin. At the same time, if you have concerns that your margin-based sales comp plan is creating unintended bad consequences, read this chapter and see if you couldn't migrate to a revenue-based sales comp design.

wealth accumulation programs as the individuals in your sales force are probably changing frequently and forget, unless you remind them.

Yes, one purpose of wealth accumulation programs is to help employees accumulate wealth, but they should also be used as a retentive tool, especially for the most vulnerable segment of your employee base; sales people. They can not only leave but also take business with them!

There are three primary components of communicating your benefits and wealth accumulation programs.

First, the programs themselves must be communicated. Obviously, the details of health, dental, FSA, HAS, 401K, stock plans, pensions, retiree medical, long term care policies, disability insurance, life insurance, tuition reimbursement, discounts on some items like cell phones, insurance, vacations, holidays, etc. The potential list is almost endless. My point is that the *complete list*, whatever it is and no matter how boring it may be, must be communicated on an ongoing basis. Not just upon hire. Employees, especially your sales force, most likely will never quite get the values they have in these programs. Never expect that the communication is done. Plan on communicating your benefits and wealth accumulation programs on an ongoing basis, forever.

*Secondly, the benefit values to employees need to be summed up, stacked in some format demonstrating the total potential value of **all** the benefits.* Especially for your sales force and the good performers therein, other companies are constantly trying to recruit your best sales employees so why not constantly try to retain them first?

Third, and this is where many companies fail miserably, communicate the long term potential values of working for your company - the wealth accumulation possibilities. Many companies never roll out a great presentation on what working for that company will look like in wealth over a career. Why not? Yes, you have to be careful and make sure you're not communicating in an unethical manner. Have your attorneys approve what you present. However, you can and must communicate the long term values of working at your company. Other companies are presenting their info to your best employees all the time, why not beat them to the punch? Or, are you concerned you can't compete from a total cash and wealth accumulation perspective with your competitors? If you don't think you can compete, you need to change that or your stars, especially in the sales force, will catch on to what other companies are offering and start looking around.

There is no less expensive or more retentive approach to retaining your best employees other than having them think, believe, and *see* that they are working for a great company and if they stay, they can accumulate wealth over time. Another way to say this is that you should overwhelm your employees with the great news of working for your company, especially the sales force. If you deliver, your employees will deliver as well and stay.

In a broad view of sales comp, I would include all of the company's benefits that a sales force is eligible to participate in.

Continually communicate all the values of working for your company (especially the long term potential wealth accumulation) – not just the commission components.

I hate using margin in sales comp plans. The craziest place to use a margin-based sales comp plan (or even a large focus on expenses) is in a company with high margins. If you have a high margin business, focus your sales team 98%, 99%, 100% on growing their revenues. If you have some sales managers who continually spend too much, work with those few sales managers. Don't redesign your sales comp plan for *everyone* to just get at just a few bad eggs. Remember some of the key premises of this book. 1. Sales comp can't do everything and 2. Have your sales management team do their job and not abdicate issues to the sales comp plan (margin or expense management in this case) that belong to sales managers.

If you use margin, see how much time is spent by your sales force trying to maximize their incomes by playing with whatever the margin is or should be. If they spend time on this area, I'd get rid of margin as a measure. Time spent inside a company and not with customers is the wrong place for your sales people to be.

With a margin design, sometimes a rep can make more money by working on how the margins are calculated inside the company then the money they can make by actually selling something to a customer. I have actually seen this happen.

Avoid margin unless you absolutely must use it - even though your CFO may disagree with this approach.

Chapter 33 - Communicating all the Values of Working for Your Company

MT. ST. HELENS was acquired by another company. The acquiring company presented their benefits package to *MT. ST. HELENS* sales force. Detail by detail by boring detail. Not one rep or sales manager interviewed after the presentations fully understood how outstanding all of the new benefits and wealth accumulation tools they now had as employees of the new compensation. What a shame. The acquiring company could have boosted morale and increased the likelihood of retaining the sales people during a time of turbulence due to the acquisition if they had truly helped *MT. ST. HELENS* sales force understand what they were getting compared to the benefits they had previously at *MT. ST. HELENS*.

One key area companies miss in communicating the values of working for their company is the "stacking" of all the values of all the benefit programs as well as longer term projections of what participation could mean for employees if the company achieved its goals.

PIKES PEAK had fabulous benefits, great wealth accumulation opportunities, and the company was growing incredibly fast. However, employee participation in the programs was terrible and for the sales force, even worse.

A six-month campaign was implemented to communicate the total values of working for *PIKES PEAK*. After six months, sales force participation in the voluntary wealth accumulation programs was reviewed and 60%+ of the sales force had either started participating or increased their participation in the wealth accumulation programs!

Constant ongoing communication of all the values of working for your company is a must. Never think you are done communicating the values of working for your company.

It gets tedious, but your sales force is constantly changing and they need a steady flow of information about your salary, benefits, and

Other Fun Stories from the Front Lines of Sales Comp

Chapter 34 - Sales Comp at Start Ups

Why do some sales people go to startups? The potential for wealth accumulation and simply, cash. The two generators of the potential wealth accumulation and cash should be over quota performance and equity when a monetizing event occurs. You don't want to attract sales people with above market "at quota" guaranteed compensation. You want the sales people to *earn* their above market compensation.

Many startups think they need to pay over market rates to get the best people. I disagree with that. You should be able to attract great sales talent at market rates if they have substantial above market opportunity *when they are over quota* and from equity participation.

At start ups, above quota payout rates can be substantially higher than at more established businesses because the base of business is so small. Once over quota, *the actual amount of revenue over quota* will also be relatively small and therefore to deliver large incomes for over quota performance, a start up will use over quota payout rates of 50%+ or more of revenue.

With that high of payout rates for over quota performance, your star performers – defined as sales people well over quota – can earn substantial commissions. That's one reason they came to the start up!

More established businesses will have payout rates over quota as low as 5% to 10% of revenue.

At times, start ups get "held up" by a few star rep performers who grow their business at a much faster rate than their peers. Then those few reps "hold up" the company or put a "gun" to the company and say, If you don't keep paying me astronomical pay, I will leave and the business will shrivel up because I am the reason we have all this business." To some extent they are right. However, if the reason they have made astronomical pay is because they have *performed over quota* and you have had a well designed sales comp plan, you don't have a problem. All they need to do is continue to perform over quota and they will continue to earn astronomical pay.

The problem occurs when your at quota compensation (or guarantee's) are substantially over market pay and the reps really haven't been performing all that well but rather have earned substantial incomes because the sales comp plan was poorly designed, they had huge guarantee's and, the initial level of at quota comp was simply too high to begin with.

Start ups are unique and it's amazing how impactful, positively and negatively, commission designs effect executive management time and literally the overall performance of a start up. If there ever is a time in the life of a company when SCME is necessary, it's in the initial phase of building a sales force.

Chapter 35 – Conclusion

I believe Sales Comp can be Made Easy. Designs can be developed that are simple, motivational, "work" for the company and sales employees, especially if the following ideas are never forgotten:

1. Have achievable quotas – if you use them.
2. Use a simple design – KISS.
3. Avoid fatal flaws.
4. Don't try to do everything with sales comp.
5. Deeply involve first line sales managers in the design process.

Go design a great sales comp plan and then watch your sales employee's meet and exceed your company's expectations.

When I design sales comp plans for companies, my design goals and process are as follows:

My Design Goals:

Have a simple design.

Design a plan that will last for several years with minimal core modifications.

Have built-in leverage, i.e. over several years, as revenue increases, sales comp costs as a % of revenue should decrease.

For fast growing companies; develop a cost effective approach to splitting territories without losing reps.

Develop designs that work, for the company, large and small territories, reward eagles, put risk on turkeys, etc.

My Design Process:

I spend time with key leaders in executive management, marketing, finance, and sales management, whoever processes commissions, and sales reps and sales managers.

I learn as much about a company as possible: anticipated growth, products, pricing, headcount, selling cycle, what makes a successful rep, successful manager, industry environment, etc.

I don't bring in any "canned" designs or approaches.
I always tell you what I think, not what I think you want to hear.

As I have said earlier, my experience has been that the right design ideas for most companies reside *inside* those companies, not in some outside person or entity. Repeating - my entire approach is based on a premise I call *Decisions Drive Design – your decisions in response to tons of questions will drive your sales comp design.*

Bottom line, sales comp can be "Made Easy" and you can do it!

Made in the USA
San Bernardino, CA
10 December 2012